Great Events

The BATTLE of HASTINGS

Written and Illustrated
by Gillian Clements

W
FRANKLIN WATTS
LONDON•SYDNEY

First published in 2001 by
Franklin Watts
96 Leonard Street
London
EC2A 4XD

Franklin Watts Australia
56 O'Riordan Street
Alexandria
NSW 2015

© 2001 Gillian Clements

The right of the author to be identified
as the author of this work has been asserted.

ISBN: 0 7496 3981 4 (hbk)
ISBN: 0 7496 4253 X (pbk)

Dewey Decimal Classification Number: 942.02

A CIP catalogue record for this book
is available from the British Library.

Series editor: Rachel Cooke
Historical consultant: Claire Edwards

Printed in Great Britain

Christmas Day 1065 was not a
happy one in London. The old
King of England, Edward the
Confessor, lay gravely ill.

Edward was worried. His land
was in danger. Normans from
France, and Danes from the North,
wanted England for themselves.

3

Outside his window, Edward could hear men working hard to finish his new abbey at Westminster. It was just like the churches Edward had seen as a boy in Normandy in France.

In only three days the great building would be consecrated to the glory of God and St. Peter.

But Edward was dying.
Memories from his long life came
back to him as he slept. He
dreamed of his boyhood in
Normandy. He had escaped there
when the Danish King, Canute,
took over England's throne – fifty
years ago!

Edward had been in Normandy
for twenty-five years. "Half my
life it seems," he mumbled
in his sleep.

He remembered the people he
had met there. One of them was
William, now the powerful Duke
of Normandy.

BANG! BANG! Masons noisily
worked at stone for the abbey.
Edward stirred. "Soon, when I am
dead," he thought, "a new king
will be crowned in my new abbey."

7

But who would the new king be? "I have no children to rule after me. In my dreams I can see England consumed by fire and sword!" he said out loud.

Edward's friends waited uneasily by his bed.

Suddenly the old King opened his eyes and stretched out his hand. "Harold Godwinson, Earl of Wessex," he said to one of his companions, "brother of my wife Edith. I name you my successor. When I die, you will be king!"

At this time, England was a land of Anglo-Saxon peoples. Earl Harold, son of Godwin, was the most powerful Anglo-Saxon in the kingdom – after King Edward. His brothers were powerful too.

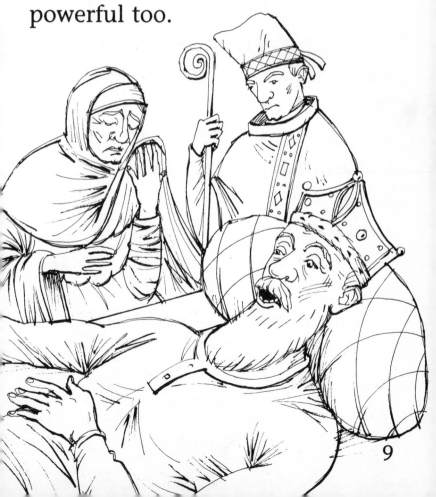

"I accept," replied Earl Harold. As he spoke, Edward closed his eyes once more and fell into a deep sleep. On 28th December Westminster Abbey was consecrated. But the King was too weak to leave his bed.

Eight days later King Edward was dead.

Harold quickly took control. "The King is dead. I am King of England now."

He knew the crown was a great prize. England was a rich land, and Edward had ruled it well enough. The towns prospered, and the land was fertile. Harold was proud to be the next king.

Edward the old King died on 5th January 1066. On the 6th he was buried in his new abbey at Westminster – and Harold was crowned there the very same day.

King Harold sat proudly on the throne. He wore his crown, and held the orb and sceptre of state firmly in his hands. "Long live King Harold," cheered the crowd.

But not everyone celebrated.

In his castle, across the Channel in Normandy, Duke William paced to and fro. He was very angry. Messengers had just arrived with news of Harold's coronation.

"I am the rightful King of England. Edward gave his word that I would be king!" he roared.

Was this true? Had Edward promised William the English throne before he gave it to Harold? No one knows for sure, although Edward had strong ties to William and to Normandy.

Duke William raged on. "The traitor Harold has broken his promise to me. I saved his life."

Two years before, Harold had crossed the sea to Normandy (no one knows why). He was captured by Guy of Ponthieu and held for ransom. William rescued Harold – and, in return, Harold swore an oath, promising to be William's loyal supporter. Later Harold said he was made to swear the oath – so it was not a true promise.

Now Harold was King of England and William could not rest. In his castle in Normandy, he sat deep in thought.

Finally he bellowed, "Call a Council of War! Fetch my brothers Robert and Bishop Odo of Bayeux. We will make our plans now."

William wanted to invade England, but he had one big problem. To defeat the Anglo-Saxons, his army had to cross the sea. "We will build a fleet of ships," he said, "large enough to carry all our soldiers, knights and horses." William needed 800 ships – so his boat builders set to work.

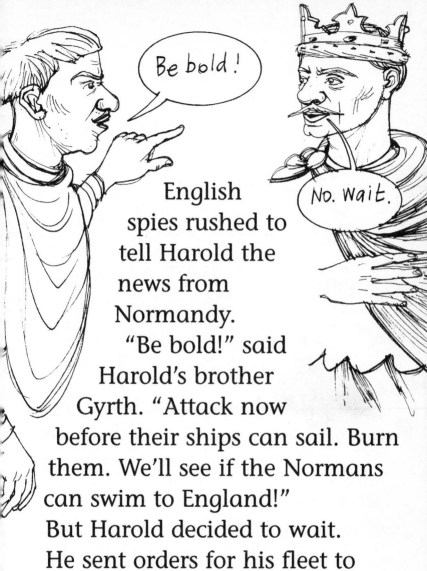

English spies rushed to tell Harold the news from Normandy.

"Be bold!" said Harold's brother Gyrth. "Attack now before their ships can sail. Burn them. We'll see if the Normans can swim to England!"

But Harold decided to wait.

He sent orders for his fleet to anchor off the Isle of Wight. They could attack the Normans when they neared the English coast.

King Harold was confident. His army was ready and mostly well trained. His best soldiers, the fierce housecarls, were armed with great battle-axes. And his Saxon peasants were ready to fight for their king.

It was 24th April. Night was falling.

Suddenly, someone pointed at the sky. "Look, a strange light in the heavens! A star with a fiery tail!" People watched in fear as a comet blazed across the sky.

"Is it a sign? Does it mean good for us? Or the Normans?" King Harold wondered. "One thing is sure, England is in danger."

The Normans were not the only threat. Harold's brother Tostig was rebellious. He had set sail to Norway, to ask King Harald Hardrada to help him fight his brother. Would Tostig raise a Norse army, and invade from the north?

"Well let them come soon..." thought Harold. "I can't fight them both at once."

By September Duke William
was ready to leave Normandy.
Tostig and Harald Hardrada's
army had already left Norway,
bound for the north of England.

King Harold had to think fast.

"We will march to Yorkshire,
and see off my brother Tostig,
and his Norse invaders!" he
declared. "Then we'll return to
face Duke William here in the
south. There is time."

In great haste the English army set off for the north. They had a long march ahead. Harald Hardrada and Tostig had landed already. Now they were marching inland.

In a few days the two forces met. The place was Stamford Bridge in Yorkshire. It was 25th September 1066. The battle was bloody. Axes and swords flashed.

One giant Norwegian warrior held the bridge for a while. He was cut down, speared through the foot from under the bridge.

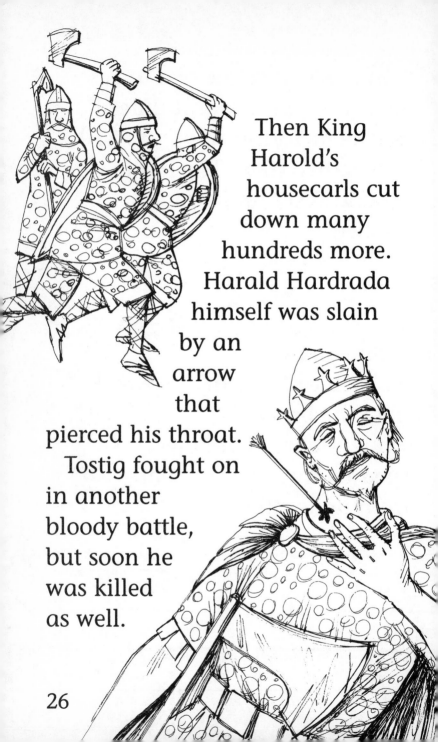

Then King
Harold's
housecarls cut
down many
hundreds more.
Harald Hardrada
himself was slain
by an
arrow
that
pierced his throat.
Tostig fought on
in another
bloody battle,
but soon he
was killed
as well.

There is no time for the spoils of war.

There was no time to celebrate the victory. "We must start at once for the south!" cried King Harold.

His peasant soldiers were exhausted. Many deserted the army and returned home. But Harold and his loyal housecarls galloped off for London. Other troops followed, gathering more volunteers on the journey south.

Meanwhile, early in the morning of 28th September, the Normans landed at Pevensey in Sussex. No one even tried to stop them. At the time, Harold's ragged army had not even left Yorkshire. "So the English have left us in peace!" smiled Duke William.

"THE NORMANS HAVE LANDED!"

A messenger met Harold on his journey south, and told him the bad news. Riding even faster, King Harold's small army reached London on 5th October. "I should have stayed down here to meet Duke William's army at the coast," Harold thought sadly.

The Norman army waited for orders. "Drag the ships ashore," shouted Duke William. "Unload the horses first. Ride east along the coast and get supplies! Build a fort at Hastings. Kill the enemy on sight. Burn their houses. Take their cattle!"

The invaders carried their cargo to dry land: wine, water and flour; spears, swords and helmets. The huge army gathered on the shore.

Duke William was happy. His army was ready. His own scouts had seen King Harold's tattered army. It was small, the soldiers and horses were tired. "Let us prepare a feast!" William cried.

Harold had left London with his brothers, Gyrth and Leofwine, and his army. There were housecarls, mercenaries, noblemen and peasants in the ranks.

For three days they marched. On 13th October, they appeared at the crest of the chalk Downs, near Hastings.

Straightaway Harold began to
organise his men along Senlac
Ridge to stop William's army
moving any further inland.

"The Normans are destroying
our land," Harold said to his
brother Gyrth. "We can't wait
for more troops. We must
fight tomorrow."

In the darkness, Harold sent his men to take up their positions on Senlac Ridge. He ordered them into a line facing south. In the front was a shield wall of housecarls. Untrained peasant soldiers lined up behind. They waited until dawn.

At first light on 14th October, the armies faced one another, armour glinting.

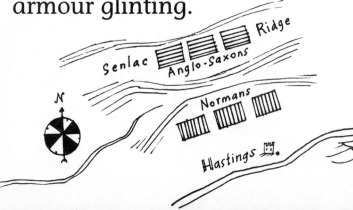

The Norman army was in
three groups on a hill below.
William was in the centre with
Bishop Odo of Bayeux at his
side. In the front were archers.
Foot-soldiers and knights were
behind.

Suddenly, shortly after 9 a.m.,
William's archers began to
move forward and fire up at the
Anglo-Saxon ranks.

Harold spoke to calm the terrified peasant soldiers: "We can beat the Norman invaders, but do not break ranks or we're lost!"

On the highest ground he set up his two standards – the "Dragon of Wessex", and "The Fighting Man". English horsemen dismounted, ready to fight on foot. Now, the real battle began.

ATTACK!

"Attack!" yelled Duke William to his men. "Have courage! We win or we die. God is on our side!"

Again the Norman archers fired arrows onto the English shield wall. But Harold's housecarls held firm. Missiles were flying from both sides.

Housecarls chopped at the Norman knights and horses as they advanced. Their axe blades flashed. "Out! Out!" they cried when the enemy fell dead.

Now some of the Normans panicked and drew back. But hot-headed English peasants chased after them down the hill. "We have won, we have won!" they cried. But they ran too far ahead, and were easily killed.

There was a pause in the fighting. Harold and William ordered their men into their battle lines again.

"Keep together," shouted Harold.

Keep together!

He knew the
shield wall must hold
to keep control of the ridge.

The attacks began again. There
was a scuffle and a shout. "Aagh!"
Duke William was thrown from
his horse. "He is dead!" the
Normans wailed. But in a second
the Duke was up. He raised his
helmet. "Victory is ahead!"
he called out.

39

Still the English shield wall held. Harold's brother Leofwine led a new attack, when SWISH! At the very worst moment, Leofwine fell dead. In fear, some of the peasants ran back.

William pressed his men on and the Norman soldiers forced the English back in bloody hand-to-hand fighting.

Englishmen were falling in terrible numbers. Both sides were exhausted. Harold prayed for nightfall, when fresh troops would arrive, but it was only two o'clock.

Then came a dreadful cry. "Gyrth has fallen!" Now both Harold's loyal brothers were dead.

Then William had a brilliant idea. He ordered his archers to shoot their arrows over the top of the shield wall and down onto English heads. The shield wall was broken. Now there was nothing to stop the Normans' advance.

Desperately King Harold and his housecarls fought on. But then a band of William's knights attacked and Harold was struck down. A lance went through his chest, then his body was hacked to pieces. The ground was stained with his blood. All was lost – all the brave housecarls were killed beside their king, along with anyone who tried to escape.

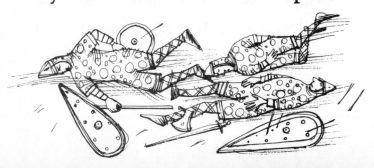

By dusk the battle was over. Harold and all his brothers were dead, and so was Anglo-Saxon England. There was no one left strong enough to stop William.

On Christmas Day 1066, in Edward's abbey at Westminster, Duke William of Normandy was crowned King William I of England – the Conqueror. He had won the Battle of Hastings. Soon he would control all of England.

In 1066, England's story changed direction. The new King's language was Norman French, not English. William's friends took over Saxon lands and Norman bishops replaced Saxon ones.

The Normans put their mark on England. They built castles and began great cathedrals.

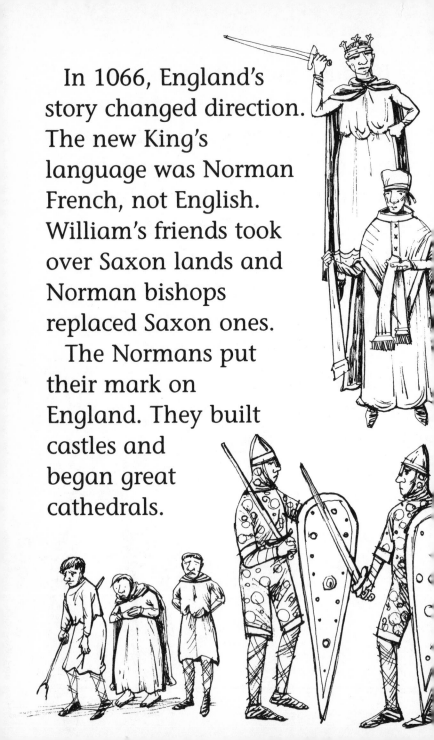

In 1086 William's servants completed the Domesday Book. In it, they listed everything William now owned in England.

His kinsman, Odo of Bayeux recorded something, too. He ordered English needlewomen to embroider a tapestry. It told the story of the Battle of Hastings – as the Normans wanted to remember it! You can still see it today in Bayeux, in France.

Timeline

1003   Edward the Confessor is born.

1013   Edward flees to Normandy as the Danes, led by Canute, fight for control of England.

1017   Canute becomes King of all England.

1028   William the Conquerer is born.

1035   William becomes Duke of Normandy. Canute dies. His son Harold Harefoot becomes King of England.

1040   Harold dies. Hardecanute, his half-brother, becomes King of England.

1042   Hardecanute dies. Edward, having returned to England, becomes King.

1045   Edward marries Edith, daughter of Godwin, Earl of Wessex, and sister of Harold Godwinson.

1051   Godwin and his sons are exiled, after rebelling against Edward, angry at his close ties with Normandy. Edward may have promised William the throne.

1052   Godwin and his sons return to England. Building of Westminster Abbey begins.

1053 Earl Godwin dies. Harold becomes Earl of Wessex.

1064 Harold goes to Normandy and is captured by Guy de Ponthieu. He is freed by Duke William and promises to support his claim to the English throne.

1065 Westminster Abbey is consecrated.

1066 **January** Edward dies. Harold is crowned king.

September Harald Hardrada of Norway invades England.

25th September Battle of Stamford Bridge. Harold defeats Hardrada.

28th September Duke William lands at Pevensey in Sussex.

5th October Harold back in London.

14th October Battle of Hastings. William defeats the English army. Harold is killed.

25th December William crowned King of England in Westminster Abbey.

1070s-80s Bayeux tapestry embroidered.

1086 The Domesday Book is completed.

Glossary

consecrate To make a place holy.

coronation The special event at which a person is crowned king or queen.

desert To run away from the army.

housecarl A soldier or bodyguard whose main job was to protect the king.

mercenary A soldier who is paid to fight for another country rather than his own.

oath A very strong promise often sworn on a sacred book such as the Bible.

peasant A person who worked on the land, farming it for a landlord, usually a noble.

rank A row of soldiers.

ransom Money paid to free a captive.

scout A person who spies on and explores an area away from the main army.

shield wall A defensive wall made by holding lots of shields together in a line.

standard A flag or banner on a pole.

volunteer A person who joins the army because they want to, not because they have to.